I0049207

PUMPKIN'S PENNIES

MARK HALLINK

SPRINGWELL
PUBLISHING

PUMPKIN'S PENNIES

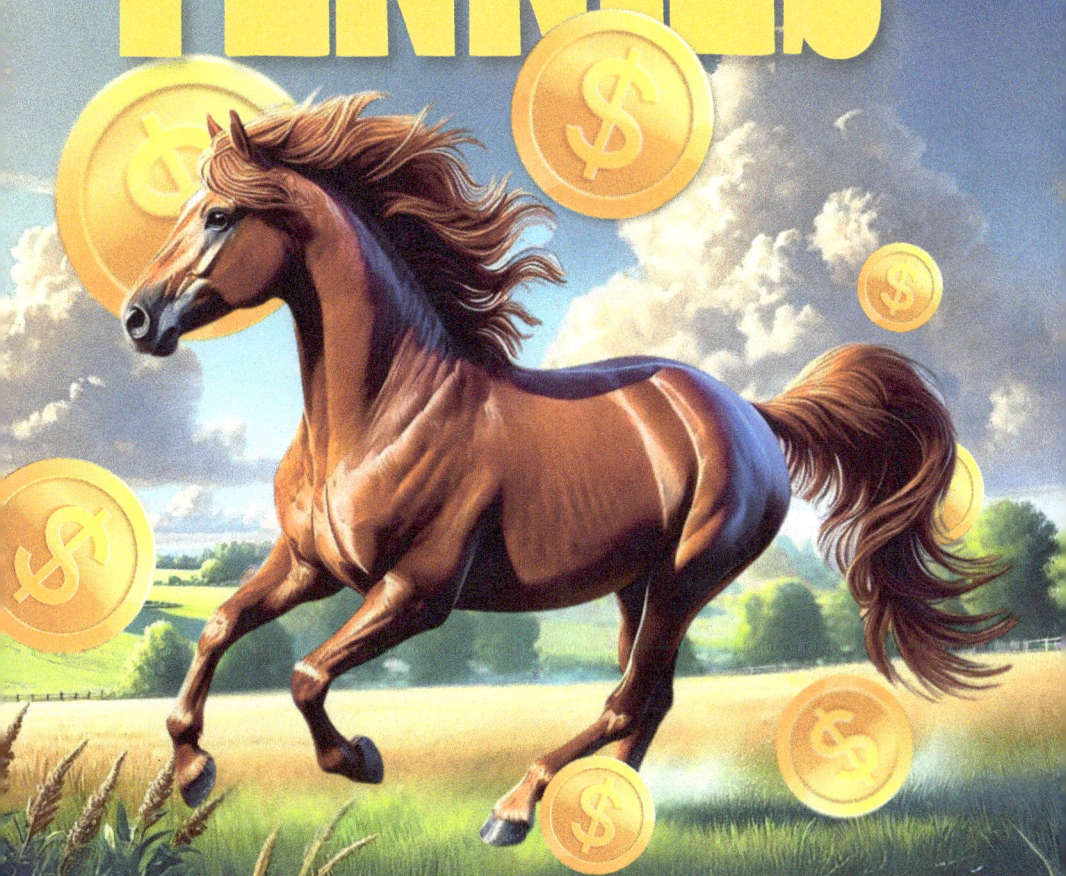

Smart Spending and Saving for Kids and Families

MARK HALLINK

Pumpkin's Pennies

© 2025, Mark Hallink

Published By: Springwell Publishing, Newberry, Florida

First Edition 1-2-3-4-5-6-7-8-9-10

All Rights Reserved

Printed in the United States

The characters and events portrayed in this book are fictitious. Any similarity to real persons, living or dead, is coincidental and not intended by the author.

No part of this book may be reproduced, or stored in a retrieval system, or transmitted in any form or by any means, electronic, mechanical, photocopying, recording, or otherwise, without express written permission of the publisher.

ISBN (Hardback): 979-8-9922405-8-0
ISBN (Paperback): 979-8-9923032-9-2
ISNB (eBook): 979-8-9922405-0-4
ISBN (Audiobook): 979-8-9923032-6-1

Illustrations by M.N.Z.V. Services

Library of Congress Control Number: 2025910811

Dedicated to our amazing grandchildren,
Layla and Kincaid

Contents

A Journey to Smart Spending and Saving

WELCOME TO SPRINGWELL FARMS, Springwell for short, a bustling farm filled with laughter, friendship, and daily adventures. Among the many animals who call Springwell home is Pumpkin, a clever and curious mare who loves exploring and learning new things.

Pumpkin is known for her sassy but kind nature, her super fast gallops across the fields, and her ever-present smile that brightens everyone's day. Like many places where friends gather, Springwell has its special way of doing things. Here, animals big and small use shiny little coins called 'horsey coins' to buy and trade for what they need.

From hay and apples to cozy blankets and stylish hats, "horsey coins" help the farm's residents get the essentials—and a few fun extras! One day, while assisting G-Pa at the market, Pumpkin noticed something that sparked her curiosity. She saw animals exchanging these shiny coins for all sorts of goods.

Some animals seemed to have many coins, while others had just a few. This made Pumpkin wonder, where do 'horsey coins' come from? How do you get them, and what is the best way to use them? Determined to find answers, Pumpkin embarked on a journey of discovery that led her through many exciting lessons about earning, saving, spending, and sharing.

Each lesson brought new challenges and joys, teaching Pumpkin —and all her friends at Springwell—the value of money and the importance of managing it wisely. So, dear readers, saddle up and join Pumpkin as she trots through fun adventures and learns smart ways to handle her 'horsey coins.'

By the end of this journey, not only will Pumpkin have discovered how to make her dreams come true, but you will also have all the tools you need to start your adventure in smart spending and saving!

1

PUMPKIN EARNS HER KEEP

PUMPKIN'S FRIENDS
AT SPRINGWELL

THIS IS RIVER!

I N THE GOLDEN LIGHT of early morning, Springwell was alive with activity. G-Pa was already out in the
fields, and Nay-Nay was tending to the horses. Among
the bustling creatures, Pumpkin, the spirited mare, was
eager to start her day. Pumpkin loved helping around the farm.

This morning, her task was to help G-Pa deliver fresh vegetables to the local farmers' market. With a sturdy cart hitched
behind her, filled with juicy tomatoes, crisp lettuces, and
plump berries, Pumpkin trotted proudly beside G-Pa down the
dusty farm road.

As they set up their stall at the market, Pumpkin watched
in fascination as animals from all over exchanged shiny horsey
coins for some of Springwell's best produce. She noticed that
every time someone made a purchase, G-Pa would carefully
count the coins and tuck them away in his worn leather pouch.
Curious, Pumpkin nudged G-Pa gently and asked, "G-Pa,
where do all these horsey coins come from? And why does

everyone want them so much?" G-Pa chuckled, patting Pumpkin's neck affectionately.

"Well, Pumpkin," he began, these horsey coins are what we use to trade for things we need or want. You earn them by providing something of value to others, like our vegetables and fruits.

"It's how we manage to keep our farm running and how we get things that we can't grow or make ourselves." Pumpkin thought about this as she watched a young foal named JG trade a few coins for a bunch of carrots.

"So, if I help around more, could I earn some horsey coins too?" she asked eagerly. "Of course, Pumpkin," replied Nay-Nay, joining the conversation with a smile. "In fact, why don't you help me at the apple stand tomorrow? If you do a good job, I'll give you your very own horsey coins to keep." Excited at the prospect, Pumpkin nodded enthusiastically. The rest of the day, she paid extra attention to how G-Pa and Nay-Nay interacted with their customers, determined to do her best to earn her very first horsey coins.

The next day, Pumpkin was as helpful as ever, learning to greet the customers warmly and even doing quick math in her head to help Nay-Nay with change. By the end of the day, her efforts paid off. Nay-Nay handed her four shiny horsey coins, and Pumpkin felt a surge of pride.

With her very own coins jingling in her small pouch, Pumpkin realized she had taken her first steps into a much larger world—a world where hard work could be exchanged for valuable coins, and these coins could open up new possibilities she had never imagined before. As the sun set over Springwell, Pumpkin dreamed of what she might do with her newly earned horsey coins.

Little did she know, this was just the beginning of her adventures in learning about money.

2

PUMPKIN'S BIG DREAM

LIVING IN THE COUNTRY

NAY-NAY AND REMI!

A S PUMPKIN AWOKE to the soft morning light filtering through the stable, her mind was filled with dreams of what she could do with her newly earned horsey coins. The previous day's hard work at the apple stand had left her with a small pouch jingling with coins, each a symbol of her efforts and dedication.

Pumpkin spent the morning trotting around Springwell, helping where she could, always with an eye on adding more coins to her collection. By midday, as she rested under the shade of a large oak tree, she thought about what she truly wanted.

It wasn't just treats or small toys. Pumpkin had a bigger dream—a cozy, warm blanket for the chilly nights. With her goal set, Pumpkin knew she needed to save her coins rather than spend them right away. She recalled watching G-Pa and Nay-Nay discussing their savings for farm improvements and how they sometimes had to wait for things they wanted.

Inspired by their discipline, Pumpkin decided to apply the

same principles. That afternoon, while Pumpkin was assisting Nay-Nay with grooming the younger foals, she shared her plan. Nay-Nay listened intently, her eyes twinkling with pride.

"That's a wonderful goal, Pumpkin," she said. "Saving for something big shows you understand the value of your hard work. And remember, every coin you save is a step closer to your blanket."

Encouraged by Nay-Nay's words, Pumpkin became even more determined. She devised a simple plan: for every ten coins she earned, she would save eight for her blanket and spend two on little necessities, like extra hay or an occasional sweet apple for a treat.

As days turned into weeks, Pumpkin's savings grew. She found joy in watching her stash increase, each coin added making her dream seem a little more achievable.

But saving wasn't always easy. There were some days when she longed to splurge on a big bag of delicious oats or a fancy new halter. Yet, the image of the cozy blanket, warm and soft, waiting to be hers, kept her super focused.

One sunny afternoon, with her goal nearly reached, Pumpkin organized a small gathering at the farm. She wanted to share her experience and teach the other animals about saving.

As they listened to her story, the animals—inspired by her dedication—began to think about their dreams and what they might also save for.

Pumpkin felt a surge of happiness, not just from her near success in saving for the blanket, but from the realization that her journey was about more than just money. It was about setting goals, making wise choices, and teaching others to do the same.

That night, as she lay in her stall, Pumpkin couldn't help but feel grateful. Grateful for the lessons learned, the coins saved, and the dreams that were slowly but surely becoming a reality.

3

THE TEMPTATION OF TREATS

PUMPKIN AND HER FRIENDS GETTING A DRINK

PUMPKIN, JG, LC AND FANCY!

O N A CRISP, sunny morning at Springwell, Pumpkin was brimming with excitement. Her pouch of horsey coins was heavier than ever, jingling merrily as she trotted about her daily chores. The warm, cozy blanket she had been saving for was almost within reach.

Just a few more coins, Pumpkin thought, and it would be finally hers. As she headed to the market with Nay-Nay to get supplies for the farm, Pumpkin's resolve was put to the test.

The market was bustling with colors and sounds, and delicious aromas wafted through the air. The tables and countertops were filled with tempting treats!

Glistening apples dipped in honey, fresh oats mixed with molasses, and crunchy carrots glazed with sugar. Pumpkin's mouth watered as she passed by each stall, and her hooves seemed to slow of their own accord. The treats called to her, each more appealing than the last. She thought of her hard-earned coins. Surely, spending just one or two wouldn't hurt?

As she hesitated, her gaze fell upon a particularly beautiful blanket displayed at a nearby stall. It was even nicer than the one she had been dreaming of, adorned with colorful patterns and lined with extra soft fleece.

The sight of it strengthened her resolve. She remembered Nay-Nay's wise words about the importance of saving and how every coin spent delayed her from reaching her goal.

With a determined nod to herself, Pumpkin turned away from the treats and continued on her path. To keep her mind off the temptation, she began a conversation with Nay-Nay about the different ways they could improve the farm with the savings they had made. Nay-Nay, noticing Pumpkin's earlier hesitation, decided it was the perfect time for a lesson. "Pumpkin," she began, "it's important to balance our wants and needs."

"Sometimes, it feels good to indulge in a treat, but we must always remember our bigger goals. It's not just about denying ourselves pleasures—it's about making smart choices and prioritizing what truly matters."

As they walked and talked, Pumpkin felt a growing sense of pride in her decision. She realized that the joy of reaching her goal would last much longer than the fleeting pleasure of a sweet treat.

By the time they returned home, Pumpkin felt wiser and more confident in her ability to make smart financial decisions. Later that evening, as Pumpkin lay in her stall, she pulled out her coin pouch and counted her savings.

She was closer now, so close to her dream. The sacrifices were worth it, she thought, as she imagined covering herself in the new blanket during the upcoming winter nights.

4

PUMPKIN'S PIGGY BANK

TRAIL RIDING WITH NAY-NAY AND G-PA

IN THE CANADIAN ROCKY MOUNTAINS

THE DAY PUMPKIN finally bought her beautiful new blanket was a day of celebration at Springwell. The vibrant orange fabric with golden trim (her favorite color is orange), was not only warm and soft but also a symbol of her hard work and smart saving. As she snuggled under it for the first time, she felt a wave of pride and accomplishment.

Her first major financial goal had been achieved. But as the excitement settled, Pumpkin found herself pondering what to do next. She still had some horsey coins left and knew she would continue to earn more. How should she manage her money now that her immediate goal was met?

Noticing Pumpkin's thoughtful expression one morning, G-Pa decided it was the perfect moment to introduce her to the next step in financial wisdom—budgeting. "Pumpkin," G-Pa began, "you've done a fantastic job saving for your blanket. Now, let's think about how you can manage your coins going forward to meet your needs and maybe even save for something else you want in the future." Together, they sat down in the barn with a large piece of paper and colorful markers. G-Pa drew three columns labeled: Savings, Needs, and Wants.

"This," he explained, "is a budget. It's a plan that helps us decide in advance how to spend our coins wisely." They started filling in the columns. Needs included her regular expenses like food and grooming supplies. Wants were the less essential items that brought her joy, like occasional treats or new tools for the farm chores.

Savings were for future goals or unexpected needs, like repairs around the farm or emergencies. Pumpkin decided to allocate a significant portion of her earnings to savings, remembering how fulfilling it felt to reach her goal. She set aside a modest amount for wants, determined to maintain her discipline. The largest share was dedicated to her needs, ensuring she could comfortably cover her daily expenses. As weeks turned into months, Pumpkin stuck to her budget with G-Pa's help. She sometimes found it challenging, especially when she passed by the market stalls filled with tempting goodies.

But the sight of her orange blanket in her stall reminded her of the rewards of sticking to a plan. One windy-rainy afternoon, a leak started in the roof of the barn. Thanks to her savings, Pumpkin was able to contribute to the repairs immediately.

This not only protected her and her friends from the elements, but also filled her with a sense of pride and independence. From that day on, Pumpkin not only saw her budget as a tool for personal savings, but as a means to contribute to the needs of Springwell. She realized that money, when managed well, could provide both personal security and community support. Through her journey with her new blanket and her budgeting efforts, Pumpkin learned valuable lessons about the power of financial planning. Her story became a favorite among the younger animals on the farm, inspiring them to start their own savings for big dreams and little comforts.

5

SHARING WITH FRIENDS

SPRINGWELL COMMUNITY

YO-YO THE DONKEY

ITH HER NEW ORANGE blanket now a cozy addition to her stall, Pumpkin enjoyed the warmth and comfort it provided every night. But more than just its physical warmth, the blanket was a constant reminder of the rewards of saving and planning.

As the days grew shorter and the air cooler, Pumpkin started to think beyond her own needs. One brisk morning, as Pumpkin and Nay Nay were preparing for the day's work, they noticed that not all the animals at Springwell were as warm and comfortable as Pumpkin. Little Joey, a young goat, struggled to stay warm during the chilly nights.

Seeing Joey shiver stirred something in Pumpkin. She remembered how her own blanket had made such a difference and thought about how she could help. With G-Pa's recent lessons in mind, Pumpkin approached him with a smile on her face. "Pumpkin," G-Pa said, noticing her thoughtful smiley look, "what's on your mind?" "I've been thinking,

G-Pa," Pumpkin began, "about how lucky I am to have my blanket. Joey and some of the others don't have anything as warm. Could I use some of my horsey coins to help them?" G-Pa smiled, his eyes twinkling with pride. "That's a very kind thought, Pumpkin. Sharing with those in need is just as important as managing our own money wisely."

Together, they planned a small project. Pumpkin would use a portion of her savings to buy materials, and with Nay-Nay's help, they would make warm covers for Joey and any other animal who needed them. Over the next few days, Springwell became a hub of activity.

Other animals, inspired by Pumpkin's generosity, offered to help too. Some contributed a few coins, others helped with sewing and assembling the covers, and some offered their stalls to store materials. As they worked together, the barn was filled with laughter and chatter, creating a sense of community and warmth that went far beyond the physical warmth the covers would provide. When the project was complete, they organized a small gathering to distribute the warm covers. Joey, receiving his new warm cover, couldn't stop bleating his thanks. The look of joy and relief on his face made Pumpkin's heart swell.

That evening, as Pumpkin lay under her blanket, she felt a warmth that came not from the fleece but from the joy of helping others. She had learned another valuable lesson— money, when used to help others, could enrich her life in ways she had never imagined. Nay-Nay came over to Pumpkin's stall, a soft smile on her face.

"You've done something wonderful, Pumpkin. You've not only kept yourself warm but have spread warmth throughout the farm. That's the true power of sharing and caring." Pumpkin drifted off to sleep, feeling more content than ever. The project had not only helped her friends but had also brought everyone closer together. She realized that the true value of money isn't just in saving or spending wisely but also in using it to make a difference in the lives of others.

6

REACHING GOALS AND BEYOND

PUMPKIN AND G-PA

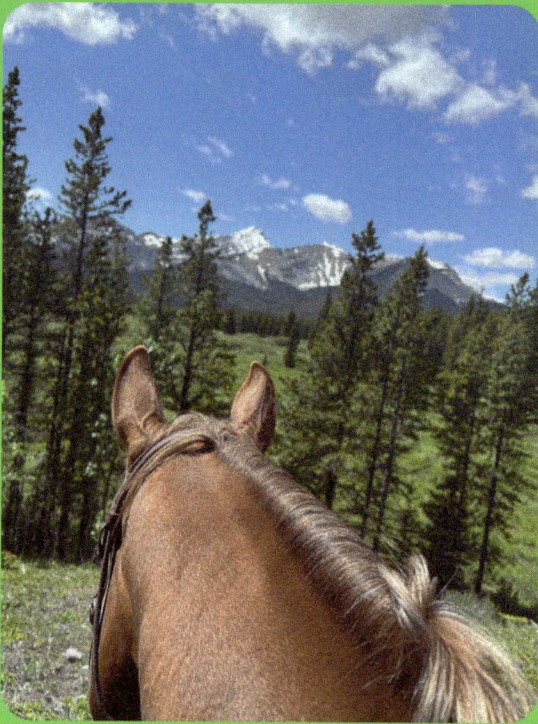

IN THE MOUNTAINS
WITH NAY-NAY

AFTER THE SUCCESS OF the community warmth project, Pumpkin felt a renewed sense of purpose at Springwell. She had seen firsthand how her financial decisions could positively affect those around her, and it inspired her to think about what she could achieve next.

As the winter thawed into spring, Pumpkin noticed the farm equipment starting to show signs of wear and tear. The wheelbarrow had a wobbly wheel, and the hay-feeder was bent pretty badly and nearly rusted through.

Remembering how everyone had come together to make the warm covers, Pumpkin wondered if she could spearhead another project—this time, to improve the tools and equipment that all the farm animals used daily. Pumpkin discussed her new goal with G-Pa and Nay-Nay one sunny afternoon. "We all benefit from the farm tools," she explained. "Maybe we can all help fix them up, just like we did with the blankets."

G-Pa nodded, impressed with Pumpkin's initiative. "That sounds like a great idea, Pumpkin. You've really taken to heart the lessons about money and community." With G-Pa's guidance, Pumpkin began to plan a fund for the farm tools.

She used the budgeting skills she had learned to set aside a part of her earnings for the equipment fund. She also talked to the other animals, explaining her idea and asking if they could contribute some of their horsey coins or time to help repair and maintain the tools. The response was overwhelmingly positive.

The animals were eager to contribute, whether by donating coins or by offering their skills. Some of the animals were good at woodworking, while others were handy with metal. Together, they had all the skills they needed to fix up anything on the farm. Over the next few weeks, Springwell was bustling with activity. The animals worked together, fixing the wheelbarrow, oiling the hinges on the barn doors, and patching up the fences. Pumpkin was right in the middle of it all, organizing the efforts and making sure everything was done right. As they worked, the animals learned new skills from each other, and the farm began to look better than ever.

The improved tools made their daily tasks easier and more efficient, which made everyone's life a little better. One evening, after a long day of work, the animals gathered around a newly repaired picnic table to share a meal. They talked and laughed under the stars, appreciating the fruits of their labor.

Pumpkin felt a deep satisfaction, not just from seeing the tangible results of their work but from knowing she had helped foster a spirit of cooperation and self-reliance among her friends. She had learned that reaching her goals didn't have to mean the end of her journey—it could also be a beginning, a way to open up new opportunities for herself and her community. As the evening wound down, G-Pa put a gentle hand on Pumpkin's back. "You've done something remarkable, Pumpkin. Not only have you reached your goals, but you've helped others reach theirs. You're a true leader." Pumpkin looked around at the smiling faces of her friends and felt an overwhelming sense of gratitude and purpose. She realized that the true joy of achieving goals lay in the journey and the people who joined her along the way.

7

TEACHING THE LESSONS BACK

MARTIN THE GOAT

PUMPKIN'S SMART GOAT PUPIL

ITH THE FARM TOOLS PROJECt successfully completed, Pumpkin became a well-respected figure at Springwell. Her journey from saving for a personal goal to leading community projects inspired many of the other animals. They saw in her not just a friend, but a mentor who could guide them in managing their horsey coins.

Observing this, Nay-Nay suggested to Pumpkin, "You've learned so much about financial wisdom, Pumpkin. Maybe you could teach the others more formally. How about starting a little school right here on the farm?" Pumpkin loved the idea. She imagined a small classroom under the big oak tree, where the sun filtered through the leaves in dappled light—a perfect setting for learning.

With G-Pa's help, they set up log benches and a large chalkboard made from an old piece of wood. They called it "Pumpkin's Pennies' School," and soon, the first class was scheduled.

The first lesson was about earning and saving horsey coins. Pumpkin shared her story of how she saved for her orange blanket, emphasizing the importance of setting clear goals. "When you know what you're saving for," Pumpkin explained, "it's easier to resist spending on things you don't really need."

As the weeks went by, Pumpkin covered more topics: budgeting, spending wisely, and sharing with others. Each lesson was filled with real examples from around the farm, making the lessons tangible and relatable. She used her experiences and those of other animals to illustrate each point, helping her classmates see how these concepts applied in their daily lives.

One particularly sunny afternoon, the lesson was on the joy of sharing. Pumpkin recounted the warm covers project and how it not only helped their friends keep warm-but also brought everyone closer together. "When we share and help each other," Pumpkin taught, "we make our whole community stronger and happier." The impact of these lessons was profound. The animals started their own little savings jars, labeled with pictures of what they were saving for. They began helping each other more, whether it was sharing food, time, or skills.

Springwell was becoming not just a place where animals lived, but a thriving community where they grew together. At the end of the season, they held a celebration to mark the end of the first 'semester' of Pumpkin's Pennies' School. G-Pa and Nay-Nay were there, beaming with pride. The other animals presented Pumpkin with a handmade medal, crafted from bits of metal and ribbon, as a token of their appreciation.

"For our teacher," they said, and Pumpkin felt her heart swell with pride and joy. That night, as she lay under her beloved orange blanket, Pumpkin reflected on her journey. From a curious mare just starting to understand money, to a teacher helping others find their path, she had come a long way. As she looked up at the stars twinkling above, she realized that teaching had taught her just as much as she had taught her friends.

8

PUMPKIN'S PENNIES' SCHOOL

WINTER LIFE AT SPRINGWELL FARM

DRIVING A SLEIGH WITH RIVER!

A S SPRINGWELL WELCOMED the fresh breeze of spring, the farm was alive with a new sense of purpose and energy. Inspired by Pumpkin's Pennies' School, many of the farm's residents were buzzing with entrepreneurial spirit, finding innovative ways to apply their lessons in financial literacy to real-world projects.

The chickens, always early risers, had started a community garden. They meticulously planted and tended to a variety of herbs and vegetables, not only to feed themselves but also to create a surplus to sell at the local market. This venture provided them with additional horsey coins and contributed to the farm's self-sufficiency.

Meanwhile, a pair of ducks took on the task of managing the farm's pond. Their project focused on keeping the water clean and supporting a healthy ecosystem, which included everything from algae control to ensuring clean water for all farm animals.

Their efforts not only improved the quality of life on the farm but also taught them valuable skills in environmental stewardship. Pumpkin, observing the success of these projects, felt a surge of pride. She realized that the financial wisdom taught at her school could have profound implications beyond individual savings.

It was about empowering each animal to contribute to the farm's overall well-being and sustainability. With the enthusiastic support of G-Pa and Nay-Nay, Pumpkin expanded the curriculum of her school. She introduced new courses like "Investing in Our Future," which encouraged animals to think about long-term benefits and sustainable practices.

Another course, "Smart Spending for a Better Farm," taught animals how to allocate resources wisely to improve their community. The newfound knowledge led to a variety of small projects that transformed Springwell. Animals learned to work together, pooling their resources and skills. A squirrel and a rabbit opened a small carpentry shop, fixing and creating tools and furniture for the farm, which reduced the need to buy these items from outside vendors. The highlight of these collective efforts was the inaugural Springwell Fair.

Organized by Pumpkin and her classmates, the fair was a showcase of innovation and collaboration. Animals from all corners of the farm came to display their projects, share their stories, and sell their goods. Workshops on topics like "Budgeting for Better Farming" and "Eco-Friendly Farming Practices" were popular attractions, drawing crowds eager to learn.

As the fair concluded, the farm community gathered to celebrate their achievements. It was a moment of reflection on how far they had come, not just in terms of financial growth but in building a resilient and supportive community.

The fair promised to be an annual event, a testament to the enduring impact of Pumpkin's teachings.

9

A COMMUNITY IN BLOOM

PASTURE LIFE

SUMMER DAYS AT SPRINGWELL!

T HE INAUGURAL SPRINGWELL FAIR had
not only been a day of celebration but a catalyst for
ongoing growth and innovation on the farm.

The success of the fair had instilled a sense
of pride and possibility in all the farm's residents, and they
were eager to keep the momentum going. In the weeks that
followed, Pumpkin saw an increase in collaborative efforts
across the farm.

Inspired by the fair, more animals began to take initiative,
starting projects that utilized their unique skills and interests.

A group of bees, for example, expanded their honey produc-
tion, which they marketed not only at the local market but also
to nearby farms.

They used their earnings to improve their hives and invest in
wildflower planting, which enhanced biodiversity and beauty
around the farm.

Similarly, a team of goats and sheep, who had learned about

sustainable grazing practices at one of the fair's workshops, began managing the farm's grasslands more effectively.

They rotated their grazing areas to prevent overgrazing and worked with Pumpkin to budget for natural fencing that would help maintain the health of the land.

As these projects flourished, Pumpkin realized the importance of sharing these successes beyond Springwell.

She started a monthly newsletter, distributed at the local market and through a network of neighboring farms, detailing the innovative projects and the lessons learned at Springwell.

The newsletter included tips on financial management, sustainable farming, and community building, extending the reach of Pumpkin's Pennies' School's teachings. The newsletter quickly gained popularity, and soon, Springwell was hosting visitors from other farms who came to learn about their initiatives.

These visits fostered a larger community of learning and sharing, which led to the establishment of the Regional Farm Network. This network facilitated regular meetings and workshops where farms could collaborate on larger projects, share resources, and support each other's growth.

The impact of these developments was profound. Springwell became a model of sustainable and financially savvy farming practices, inspiring similar transformations in the wider agricultural community.

Pumpkin, witnessing the ripple effects of her school's teachings, felt an immense sense of fulfillment.

She had not only transformed her own farm but had also played a part in promoting broader changes that benefited many.

10

LESSONS IN ENTROPY AND LUCK

CHASE

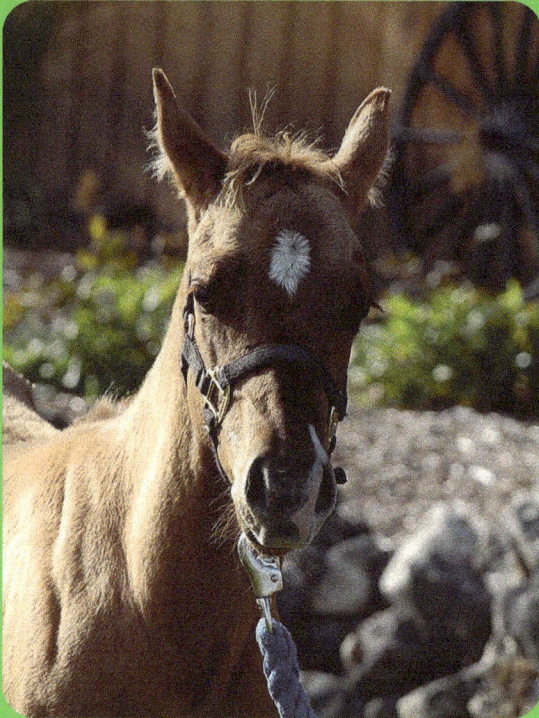

GROWING UP!

AS SPRINGWELL FLOURISHED with new projects and partnerships, Pumpkin found herself reflecting on some of the more subtle lessons she had learned along the way—those of entropy and luck. She realized these forces played just as crucial a role in their lives as the financial lessons she had taught.

One quiet evening, as Pumpkin and her friends gathered around a newly built fire pit, she decided to introduce these concepts. "Tonight, I want to talk about two things that affect us all, though we often don't see them: entropy and luck," Pumpkin began, her audience listening intently. "Entropy is a fancy word for poop happens" she explained.

"It's like when we clean our stalls, and somehow, by the next day, they're messy again. It happens in our financial lives too. We plan and save, but unexpected expenses—like a broken fence or a sick friend—can disrupt those plans."

To help illustrate her points, Pumpkin used a simple

analogy: "Think of entropy like this," she started, drawing their attention to a small pile of beautifully stacked hay bales next to a scattered pile. "When we stack these hay bales neatly, they are in order. It takes energy and effort to stack them up.

"But over time, as we take hay from the stack to eat or it gets bumped, the pile starts to spread out and becomes messy. This spreading out, or moving towards disorder, is entropy at work." Pumpkin continued, "In our savings and spending, entropy appears when unexpected expenses come up.

"For example, if we don't plan for things like a storm damaging the barn roof or the need to replace old tools, our financial order can become disorderly. Our savings might disappear faster than we planned." She also highlighted that managing financial entropy isn't just about fixing things when they break.

"It's also about regular checks and balances," she noted. "Just like how we might tidy our stalls regularly to keep them from becoming too chaotic, frequently reviewing our budget and adjusting our savings can help us manage financial entropy. It keeps our financial goals on track and prevents disorder from derailing them.

"Entropy is a fancy word for the chaos and disorder that seems to naturally happen," she explained. "It's like when we clean our stalls, and somehow, by the next day, they're messy again. It happens in our financial lives too. We plan and save, but unexpected expenses—like a broken fence or a sick friend—can disrupt those plans."

Then, she shifted to the idea of luck. "Luck, on the other

hand, can sometimes bring good things our way when we least expect it. Like finding an extra bunch of carrots in the market, or a new friend who brings new opportunities.

"But," she cautioned, "relying on luck isn't a plan. We should enjoy it when it comes but always prepare as if it won't. Because often, what looks like luck is really just the outcome of diligent effort and readiness aligning with the perfect opportunity."

The animals learned that while entropy and luck could not be controlled, their effects could be managed through smart planning and preparation. This understanding empowered them to take proactive steps towards maintaining order and seizing opportunities as they arose.

As another year passed, the second annual Springwell Fair was even more successful than the first. It celebrated not only the achievements within Springwell but also those of the entire Regional Farm Network. The fair had grown into a regional event, drawing attention from far and wide, showcasing how community-focused financial literacy could lead to substantial and sustainable growth.

Under the shade of the big oak tree, where it all began, Pumpkin looked out over the bustling fair, her heart full. She knew that the seeds of knowledge and collaboration she had planted had grown into a thriving ecosystem of shared prosperity. Her journey had taught her that with curiosity, education, and community, there was no limit to what could be achieved.

THE END

NOW FOR SOME MORE OF PUMPKIN'S FRIENDS...

DAISY THE DOG

THE NEIGHBORS

YO-YO AND BABY JO-JO

MORE PUMPKINS WITH K!

LAYLA AND ELSIE!

SPICEY

Afterword

As the author of "Pumpkin's Pennies: A Journey to Smart Spending and Saving," I've endeavored to weave together a narrative that not only entertains but educates. The story of Pumpkin, a mare with a curiosity as vast as her heart, was born from a combination of my life experiences and a strong desire to teach the principles of financial literacy in a manner that resonates with readers of all ages.

From hay and apples to cozy blankets and stylish hats, 'horsey coins' help the farm's residents get the essentials—and a few fun extras! One day, while assisting G-Pa at the market, Pumpkin noticed something that sparked her curiosity. She saw animals exchanging these shiny coins for all sorts of goods.

Writing this book has been a journey of exploration—into the simplicity of storytelling and the complexities of financial management. Pumpkin's adventures are more than just children's tales; they are lessons in prudence, responsibility, and the joys of wise financial decisions. My hope is that young readers will find inspiration in Pumpkin's determination and creativity as she learns to manage 'horsey coins' and navigate through her challenges.

This book is also a reflection of my personal philosophy that learning should be engaging and accessible. By personifying financial concepts through Pumpkin and her friends at Springwell Farms, I've aimed to present economic principles in a digestible and relatable way. Initial feedback from early readers, who have expressed a newfound interest in saving and budgeting, confirms that Pumpkin's lessons are hitting home.

Revisions throughout the writing process were guided by these young readers' insights and the invaluable feedback from various friends and family members who emphasized the importance of actionable financial knowledge. The evolution of this short book into its final form was a testament to the collaborative spirit that this project engendered.

"Pumpkin's Pennies" is not just a book but a stepping stone for many to a future where they are empowered to make informed financial decisions.

As I close this chapter in Pumpkin's story, I look forward to hearing how her lessons continue to inspire and educate, fostering a generation that approaches financial health with confidence and curiosity.

Mark Hallink

Acknowledgments

First and foremost, I extend my deepest gratitude to my wonderful and patient wife, Alice, whose undying support and love have been my anchor and inspiration throughout the writing of this book. Alice, your unwavering encouragement and the countless ways you assist me daily have made all the difference. This journey would not have been as joyful nor possible without you by my side.

I must also express my appreciation for the plethora of online tools that have significantly enhanced my research and writing process. These digital resources have been indispensable, not only for drafting and refining my manuscript but also for connecting with talented individuals, such as the voice actors who brought the audio version of this book to life. The availability and accessibility of such tools have truly transformed the creative landscape for writers everywhere.

We'd Love to Hear Your Thoughts!

If you have enjoyed reading this book or have any feedback, we'd greatly appreciate your review on Amazon. As a new author your feedback is incredibly important and very much appreciated. Thank you for your support and for helping to spread the word!

Please scan the QR code below to leave a review.

About the Author

Mark Hallink and his wife, Alice, are "trailblazers" in the world of Cowboy Mounted Shooting and dedicated advocates for the sport. As the first man and woman in Canada to achieve Men's Level Six (M6) and Ladies' Level 6 (L6) respectively, the highest ranks in the discipline, Mark and Alice's accomplishments have inspired countless enthusiasts to pursue their own riding and shooting goals.

Professionally, Mark was the founder and former president of Hallink RSB Inc., a leading innovator in the tooling and packaging industry. His company played a key role in advancing technology and design in many of the products found on grocery store shelves, setting industry standards for quality and efficiency. After selling the company in 2020, Mark transitioned into retirement, where he now focuses on his passions: writing and spending time with the love of his life, Alice, and his favorite horse, Pumpkin. Mark studied at the University of Waterloo in Canada, earning an Honours Degree in Psychology. Mark's writing spans topics like financial literacy, where he shares his expertise in business and entrepreneurship, as well as fiction, where he explores imaginative stories inspired by his experiences and love for adventure.

His work reflects his belief in perseverance, financial independence, and the joy of creative expression. Mark and Alice are retiring to North Florida, where they plan to embrace the region's natural beauty, friendly people, and continue their equestrian pursuits, exploring new adventures around the world.